praise for shaffer's books

Like a terrible accident scene that I felt ashamed for staring at […] except the book was funny and accident scenes aren't.

— A Bookish Butterfly

Andrew Shaffer is a mood.

— Bookstagram of Mine

This book made me infertile. It was either this book or the vasectomy I had around the same time I was reading it.

— Bob Lingle, Good Neighbor Bookstore

I'm not a "laugh out loud" kind of person, but Andrew Shaffer had me giggling at work while trying to pretend I was actually working.

— Books Anxiety

You're not funny and if I ever met you I would punch you in the face.

— Amazon Customer

also by andrew shaffer

POETRY

Let's See Them Poems
Look Mom I'm a Poet (and So is My Cat)
The Summer of '82 (I Still Like Beer)

FICTION

Ain't Got Time to Bleed • Catsby: A Parody
The Day of the Donald • Feel the Bern
Fifty Shames of Earl Grey • Fifty Shames Gone Grey
Ghosts from Our Past • Hope Never Dies
Hope Rides Again • How to Survive a Sharknado
Justin Bieber: First Tweets 2 Forever: My Memoir: A Parody
Mothman's Merry Cryptid Christmas
Secret Santa • The Telltale Hardon and Other Perversions

NONFICTION

Great Philosophers Who Failed at Love
*It's Beginning to Look a Lot Like F*ck This*
Literary Rogues: A Scandalous History of Wayward Authors
Oh My Goth: Jokes for When You Feel Dead Inside

ANDREW SHAFFER

NOT TODAY, SATAN
(MAYBE TOMORROW)

8TH CIRCLE PRESS

NOT TODAY, SATAN (MAYBE TOMORROW) copyright © 2023 Andrew Shaffer

All rights reserved. Any resemblance between the characters and incidents described in this book and real people is either coincidental or used fictitiously.

The text in this book was generated, edited, and proofed by human beings.

"Black Hole Heart" previously published in *Oh My Goth: Jokes for When You Feel Dead Inside* (8th Circle Press). "The Madman and the Professor" and "Review of 'Two Assholes,' an Adult Video About an Alien With Two Butts" previously published in the chapbook *Let's See Them Poems* (8th Circle Press).

Cover illustration by Marisoo. Several of the interior flower illustrations are based on stock art by Lisima, licensed via Shutterstock.

No part of this book may be reproduced in any form or by any electronic, mechanical, or magical means, without written permission from the author, except for the use of brief quotations in a book review.

Trade Paperback ISBN: 978-1-949769-55-5

Also available as an eBook

Published by 8th Circle Press (Louisville, KY) / Distributed by Ingram

For everyone who told me there was no money in poetry…
you were right.

All bad poetry springs from genuine feeling.

— OSCAR WILDE

contents

After the Break-up	1
He was a Precious Metal—	2
Her Madness	4
Can We Please Stop Using the Word "Crazy"?	5
The Last Temptation of Little Debbie	7
In the Twilight	8
All for You, My Love	10
The Six Saddest Words in the English Language	11
Live Free or Die	12
The Only Thing	15
Magic	16
Travel Advice	18
Only God Can Judge Me	19
Search Results	20
Review of "The Subtle Art of Not Giving a F*ck"	22
21st Century Lennon	23
I'm Not Crying, You're Crying	24
Humblebrag	26
About a Girl	27
Fashion Advice	28
All the Sausage Your Heart Desires	30
The Merchant of Venice Beach	31
Unsolved Mysteries	33
Dear Penthouse Review…	35
A Few Words of Advice	38
Midwest Love Poem	40
The Madman and the Professor	41
Under the Covers	42
#SponsoredPoem	45

This Poem Stinks	46
Let Her Go	47
Words are Mightier Than Swords	48
Florida	50
Rejection Letter for "Dear Penthouse Review…"	52
Black Hole Heart	53
Nature Walk	54
The Poets Strike	56
Fragile Things	59
#SponsoredPoem	61
Exact Change Only	63
You are Not a Mermaid	65
Response to "Rejection Letter for 'Dear Penthouse Review'"	66
Writing Advice	67
Shoot for the Stars	69
Review of "Two Assholes," an Adult Video About an Alien With Two Butts	71
#SponsoredPoem	72
My 21st Birthday	76
Never Stop Learning	77
Unsolicited Observation	79
Red Flag	80
Happiness is Just Around the Corner	82
Don't Panic	83
How to Be the Best "You" You Can Be (In 13 Easy Steps)	84
Liar	86
Possession	87
We are All Stardust	88
Response to Response to "Rejection Letter for 'Dear Penthouse Review…'"	91
Acknowledgments	93
About the Author	95

not today, satan

(Maybe Tomorrow?)

after the break-up

"There are plenty of fish in the sea,"
you said, hoping to cheer me up.

Thanks, I'll keep that in mind
if I ever decide to start
fucking fish.

he was a precious metal—

not silver, gold, or platinum,
but one of the mildly
radioactive ones
like uranium
which you need to
give your hands a good scrub
after touching,
but also fine
if you're into
toxic human garbage

her madness

like an idiot taking a selfie on a cliff
she got too close to the edge

and

        fell

                off

                        (splat)

can we please stop using the word "crazy"?

It trivializes the seriousness of mental illness
and contributes to harmful stereotypes,
the crazy guy shouted
as I ran from him
and his knife.

the last temptation of little debbie

Christmas Tree Cakes half off, the sign read.

Not today, Satan.
Not today.

in the twilight

Some things are so far beyond
our limited human
understanding
it's just best
to admit
we're
ignorant
and accept
we may never
know exactly why
Bella chose Edward over Jacob

all for you, my love

I don't write poetry
for the money,
the women,
the fame

I write it for you—

the obsessed, deranged fan
who has me locked
in her she-shed

I'm running out of words
to describe the terror

somebody help
call 911 and ask them
                to bring me
                        a thesaurus

the six saddest words in the english language

WE

ARE

OUT

OF

PUMPKIN

SPICE

live free or die

Underwear is just a facemask
   for your butt.

If I don't want to wear it in Costco,
   that's my freedom.

#mybuttmychoice

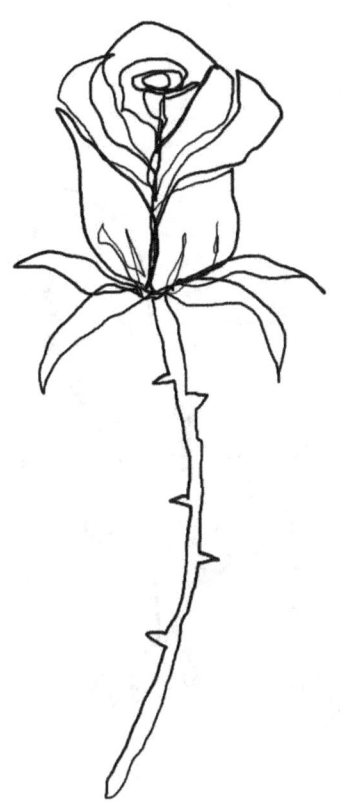

the only thing

*the only thing
that could
make her
happy
was the
one thing
she could
never have*

(a pet dinosaur)

magic

She was made of magic

    that only I could see

        which is why

            they had to put me

                on Lithium

travel advice

No matter how far you go
down the wrong road,
you can always
turn back.

Unless your engine stalls
in the middle of Nowhere, Arkansas
and a clan of hillbilly cannibals eats you.

only god can judge me

Haters will say
this isn't a poem

search results

does lana del rey
    does lana del rey have
    does lana del rey have kids
    does lana del rey have an instagram
    does lana del rey have a sister
    does lana del rey have a grammy
    does lana del rey have daddy issues

I was searching for "cats."

And the answer is yes. She has two cats.

review of "the subtle art of not giving a f*ck"

I have long been puzzled by this book—
if you truly "didn't give a fuck,"
you wouldn't use an asterisk
in the fucking title,
would you?

21st century lennon

Imagine

how much easier

it would be

to meet people

if our hearts

had Bluetooth

i'm not crying, you're crying

Tear-
drops
are just
wet feelings
that come out
of your eyeballs
when you're all
all out of
words

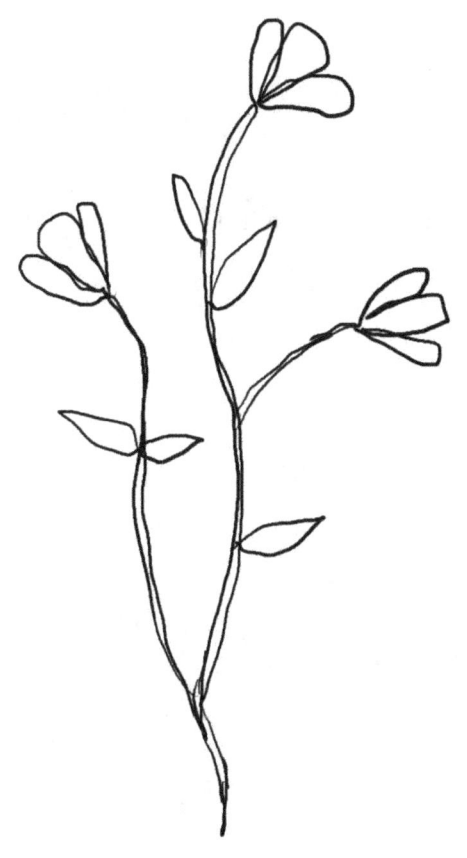

humblebrag

my penis is like a Judd Apatow movie—

                          too long, and only

occasionally

        funny

about a girl

I opened the door
and you were
standing
there
in tears,
asking if I
could find
it in my heart
to forgive you for
        shitting
            on
                my
                    waterbed

(I could.)

fashion advice

Sure, laugh at my cargo shorts.

The more pockets you have, the more
airplane bottles of Fireball Whisky
you can carry to your son's
morning soccer practice.

all the sausage your heart desires

read the menu's description of the Sausage Lover's Supreme ® pizza. Really, Pizza Pit? All the sausage thine heart doth desire? Call the slaughterhouse for back-up, because the sausage party is about to begin.

the merchant of venice beach

Act I, Scene i

Enter Antonio and Lorenzo.

ANTONIO Wherefore art thou headed this fine day, Lorenzo?

LORENZO Gold's Gymnasium. Wouldst thou like to accompany me?

ANTONIO Doth thou even lift, bro?

LORENZO 'Tis not unknown to me.

ANTONIO Come, Lorenzo; I know'st thou well.
Thou art like one of these droning fellows
That brazenly boast about thy "gains"
But art a flab-skinned nutter-butter.

LORENZO I would entreat you, friend,
To stay thy tongue, lest you lose it.

ANTONIO Ha! Tell me this, my manly brethren:
Hath thou been skipping both leg *and* arm days?
What doth thou bench?

LORENZO Three-twenty.

ANTONIO Donkey whistle!

LORENZO I do not wish to quarrel with thee, but
Thou refuseth to quench your pernicious rage.
Gentle Antonio, put thy meat-hooks up.

ANTONIO Have at thee, thou yellow led-better.

Lorenzo lowers his head and spears Antonio to the ground, where Lorenzo twists Antonio's wrist and forearm back at an unnatural angle using a Kimura Lock submission.

LORENZO Doth thou submit…bro?

ANTONIO Go fornicate with thyself.

Lorenzo tightens the Kimura Lock, wrenching Antonio's arm out of his socket in one swift movement. A sickening pop is heard.

ANTONIO [*weeping*] I concede; thou art a beast.
Let us go to the gymnasium and pumpeth iron.

Lorenzo helps Antonio to his feet. They exit.

unsolved mysteries

All this beauty in the world
and he could not stop
from staring at her,
wondering why
she had pierced
her anus

dear penthouse review...

I oft thought haughty sex poems were but fiction—
such erotic escapades were unknown frontiers
to one such as I, a New York cab driver…

…until late one Tuesday night I saw you—
flagging me down, outside
the Strand bookstore.

You had the tight body of a young Helen Mirren
and the unbridled sexual energy
of an old Helen Mirren.

I rolled down the passenger window. *Where you headed, babe?*

You bent over, your low-cut cami
giving me a nice peek at your
~~boobies~~. Brontë sisters.

Park Avenue, you said with a purr. *A little place called*

FUCK TOWN

**Population:
Me and You**

That past Midtown? I asked. *What's the cross-street?*

You ran your tongue slowly over your lips and said:

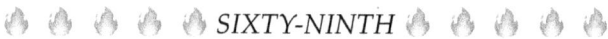

I shook my head. *Sorry, babe, my shift's almost up and that's too far north for me.*

Sometimes, late at night when the stars go dark,
I lather myself with scented oils of the Orient
and think of Emily and Charlotte. (.) (.)

and wonder
        if you ever
                made it
                        to Fuck Town.

a few words of advice

When Uncle Ben told Peter Parker, "With great power comes great responsibility," I really doubt he meant, "If you ever get bitten by a radioactive spider, put on tights and punch criminals in the face." He probably just meant be careful with the weed eater and don't lop off your ding-dong, son.

midwest love poem

Sometimes you can find what you're looking for
in your own backyard
if what you're looking for
is rhubarb

the madman and the professor

is the name of a major motion picture starring Mel Gibson and Sean Penn.

Was the title *Two Assholes* not available?

under the covers

I will never forget those long enchanted nights
we laid together naked in bed,
my ravenous lover and I,
watching cat videos
on her iPhone

#sponsoredpoem

If cowboys had wings,
they wouldn't need
horses

Ambien.

*Stop thinking
and start sleeping.*

this poem stinks

|
|
|
|
|
all she
wanted
was an Uber
that didn't have
sixteen pine-scented
air fresheners dangling
from the rearview mirror
to cover the smell of weed
was that too
much to ask?

let her go

AND IF SHE RUNS

TO THE COPS

IT WASN'T

MEANT

TO BE

words are mightier than swords

Unless
the words are
"Please put down
that ninja sword, Greg."

florida

Kids don't get snow days in Florida
and that makes me super sad
because hurricane days
just aren't the same

But they do have alligators
in swimming pools
so that's cool
I guess?

rejection letter for "dear penthouse review..."

the PARIS REVIEW

Thank you for allowing us to consider "Dear *Penthouse Review...*"

The name of our literary magazine is *The Paris Review,* NOT *The Penthouse Review.*

Unfortunately, this submission does not meet our current needs. We wish you the best of luck placing it elsewhere.

—*The Editors*

P.S. There is no business by the name of "F*ck Town" in Manhattan.

black hole heart

What's that
thing called where
your crush likes you
back? Oh, yeah—
a fantasy.

nature walk

Next time
    you're in
        the woods
            at the edge
                of the pond,
            stop walking
        and listen—
    if the woods
are quiet
enough
    and your
        mind is
            clear
                you might
                    just hear
                your phone
            buzzing

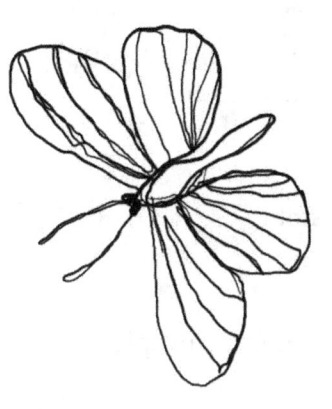

the poets strike

While making signs out of posterboard,
the first indications this endeavor is
doomed begin to emerge.

The words, they flow too easily.
To ask a poet not to use her natural gifts
is a losing game.

A few witty lines form an epigram.

One poet divides
seventeen syllables in
a three-line structure—

a grade-school attempt at haiku,
but a haiku nonetheless.

And then the rhyming begins;
oh God, the rhyming.

First two words here and there;
then the lines begin to pair

into rhyming couplets and stanzas
and then shit really gets bananas.

Do you see that sign with nothing on it?
Watch as fourteen lines cluster together,
a model Shakespearean sonnet
written in iambic pentameter.
A nineteen-line villanelle sprouts intact
and art more lovely than a summer's day
but is crushed by an absolutely stacked
twenty-five line rondeau redoublé.
One poet tosses off rhyme's tight shackles
by unearthing a rarely used schema;
and their sign positively crackles
with a wild thirty-nine-line sestina.
And just when it seems it can't get much worse,
all hell breaks loose with the dawn of free verse.

It's every poet for themselves—
without
               regard for

form
                                       rhythm
               function
or punc-
        tu-
ation.

The strike goes nowhere,
quietly petering out

               not

                        unlike

                                this

                                         poem

fragile things

Be gentle with me,
she said—
this is my first
splenectomy

#sponsoredpoem

So many poems about whiskey,
so few about cheap vodka.

And look—I get it.
Cheap vodka isn't aged in oak barrels;
it doesn't have notes of vanilla and citrus.

That thirteen-dollar bottle of Smirnoff's
doesn't "taste of her amber lips"
or "reveal unspoken
truths."

It will never "burn like candlelight in your heart"
or "warm your weathered soul"
(although it is flammable).

There is nothing remotely "magical" about it,
unless you count its singular ability
to make seventeen years
of sobriety disappear
in an instant.

And yet.

Every bottle of cheap vodka
is a lottery ticket—
will this night end
in adventure
or regret?

Smirnoff Vodka.

Where will YOU wake up tomorrow?

exact change only

You can touch my soul
 for a quarter

you are not a mermaid

Just because you dyed your hair blue
doesn't mean you're a mermaid

It just means your parents
never paid you enough
attention as a child, Karen

response to "rejection letter for 'dear penthouse review'"

Dear Editors of *The Paris Review*:

My apologies.

Sincerely,

[signature]

Andrew Shaffer

P.S. The name of the business is not "F*ck Town." It is "Fuck Town."

writing advice

Don't.

shoot for the stars

If you miss, well, don't worry.
Your bullet will eventually come down
and hit ~~someone~~ something.

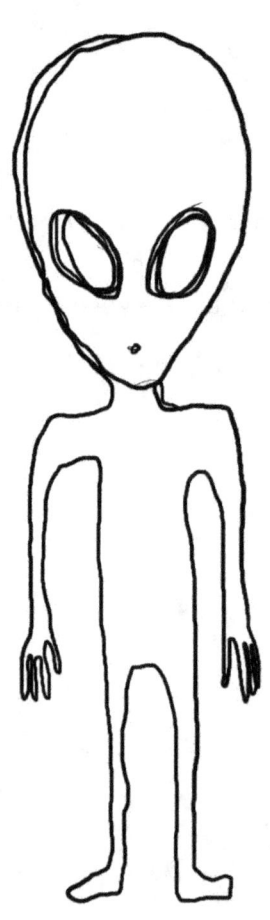

review of "two assholes," an adult video about an alien with two butts

This isn't Intro to
Extra-Terrestrial Sexuality,
this is a master class
in eating alien ass.

— Adult Video News

#sponsoredpoem

He takes one look at the true crime book
I'm reading and snorts.

"Ted Bundy is the Backstreet Boys of
serial killers," he says. "A fad."

Ted Bundy confessed to killing
thirty women in seven states.

"Only twenty are confirmed," he says.
"Not enough to crack the top ten."

If you're going by numbers alone, fine.
But to dismiss Bundy as a "fad"?

I'll grant you he doesn't have
the mystery of the Zodiac Killer.

He wasn't a pioneer like Ed Gein,
or a tastemaker like Dahmer.

He didn't create the widespread panic
of a Richard Ramirez in his prime.

The public's fascination with Bundy? Probably
more about his looks than anything else.

If that makes him the boy band
of serial killers, so be it.

What I take offense at, sir, is your baseless
assertion that the Backstreet Boys are a fad.

Since you appear to be a numbers guy,
let's take a look at the numbers:

One Direction, *NSYNC, New Kids—
they all sold a few records. (Seventy million.)

But the Backstreet Boys?
130 million.

You don't sell 130 million records
on looks alone.

Crank up "Everybody (Backstreet's Back)"
and try to tell me that doesn't still slap.

Listen to "Show Me the Meaning of Being Lonely," what many consider their crowning achievement.

If that song doesn't bring a tear to your eye, you're as much of a monster as Ted Bundy.

The Backstreet Boys have been going strong for thirty years and continue to sell out stadiums.

They show no signs of slowing down—their last album hit number one in twenty-six countries.

Does that sound like a "fad" to you?

*The Backstreet Boys 30th Anniversary Tour.
Tickets available now at all Ticketmaster locations.*

my 21st birthday

— What's your name?
— Chuck E. Cheese.
— Your real name.
— Charles Entertainment Cheese.
— I'm serious. Let me see you.
— I can't take the head off when there are kids around.
— Isn't it depressing, celebrating all these birthdays every day?
— I grew up in an orphanage. I never knew my birthday, so I celebrate everyone else's.
— Is that true?
— It's what we're supposed to say.
— Huh. Well, it's my birthday today. Do big kids get something special on their birthdays? Like a free beer?
— (whispers) If you wait until we close, Chuck E. will give you a free birthday lapdance.
— With the head on and everything?
— With the head on and everything.
— HAPPY BIRTHDAY TO ME.

never stop learning

I was thirty-nine when I finally realized
Miami rapper Flo Rida's name
was the word "Florida"
split in two.

unsolicited observation

Her mug said MALE TEARS
but she was the only one
I ever saw crying
into it

red flag

let me show you the shape of my heart, she said, sketching a medical diagram for me

the human heart has four chambers, and on one of the lower ones she'd drawn a tiny door

that's where kyle lives, she said

i asked if she was still in love with kyle and she said, *no, he's just this little guy who happens to live inside my heart*

i checked with a friend in med school who confirmed my suspicions—such a thing wasn't possible—but it wasn't a dealbreaker because, hey, we all have our quirks, right?

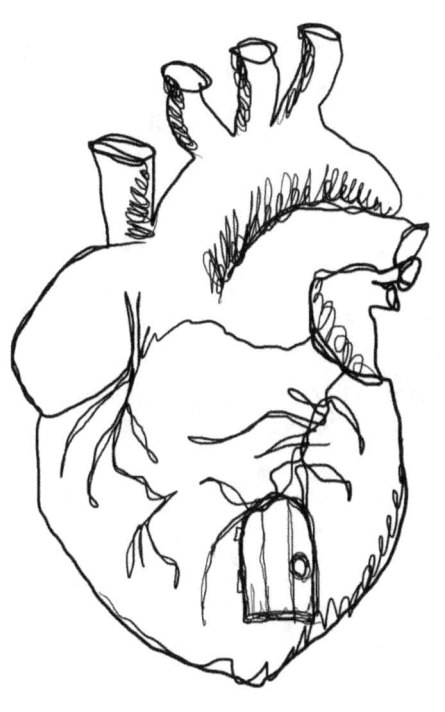

happiness is just around the corner

After a lifetime of
being told
to smile,
she was finally
grinning ear-to-ear
thanks to the mortician

don't panic

DROWNING

IS JUST

A SIGN

THAT

YOU'RE

THIRSTY

how to be the best "you" you can be (in 13 easy steps)

1. Exercise regularly.
2. Your subconscious is wise. Trust your instincts.
3. Drink plenty of water.
4. Go to the zoo.
5. Make sleep a priority.
6. Why do penguins smell so bad? Sure they eat raw fish but good lord.
7. Keep a journal.
8. Did that penguin make a snide remark under his breath?
9. Be thankful.
10. Yeah, that penguin is talking smack. Watch your mouth, buddy.
11. My mother does WHAT? OH HELL NO IT'S ON YOU FLIGHTLESS LITTLE FUCK.
12. Call your AA sponsor and ask if he can loan you seventy-five bucks for bail.
13. Eat more fruits and veggies.

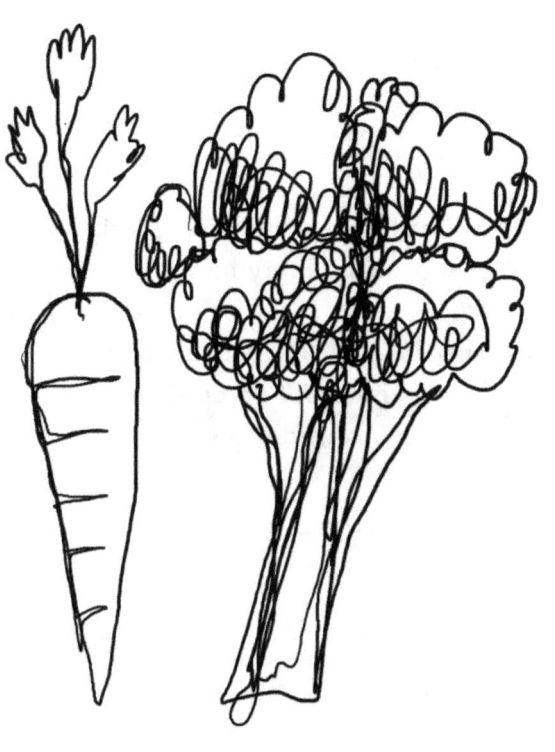

liar

"Nothing bad can happen to a writer,"
Philip Roth said. "Everything is material."

Then he died, and—to be frank—
his output dropped
considerably.

possession

In the depths of her darkest despair
she let her demons take over—
and they told her to do
all sorts of weird shit
like speak in tongues
and vote for third
party candidates

we are all stardust

except for Wonder Woman,
who was sculpted in clay
by Hippolyta, Queen
of the Amazons
of Themyscira
and brought to life
by the ancient Greek gods
which is an awkward conversation
to have with your daughter when she
asks why she doesn't have a belly button

response to response to "rejection letter for 'dear penthouse review...'"

the PARIS REVIEW

Our fucking apologies.

—*The Editors*

acknowledgments

Thank you to my wife, who did not flinch when I said, "I've decided to become the world's greatest living poet."

about the author

ANDREW SHAFFER is the *New York Times* bestselling author of the poetry collection *Look Mom I'm a Poet (and So is My Cat)* and, most recently, *Feel the Bern: A Bernie Sanders Mystery*. He lives in Louisville, Kentucky, where he is at work on a mullet.

more by andrew shaffer

"Like a terrible accident scene that I felt ashamed for staring at [...] except the book was funny and accident scenes aren't. Also, what a cute cat!" — *A Bookish Butterfly*

Shaffer's debut poetry collection features explorations of our modern world from Fortnite ("I don't care") to pretentious Instagram poets ("Lord Byron would have drunk wine from your hipster skull").

more by andrew shaffer

Even the most jaded of Hot Topic clerks will crack a smile at this morbidly funny joke book compiled by *New York Times* bestselling humorist and low-key goth Andrew Shaffer.

This illustrated collection is perfect for Halloween—or anytime, really, since true goths know that every day is Halloween.

www.ingramcontent.com/pod-product-compliance
Lightning Source LLC
Chambersburg PA
CBHW052130110526
44592CB00013B/1831